UNLEASHING YOUR INNER POWER

Unleashing Your Inner Power

A Journey to Self-Discovery

B. VINCENT

QuillQuest Publishers

CONTENTS

| 1 |

Chapter 1: Introduction

Meaning of Internal Power

As we continued looking for self-awareness and self-satisfaction, understanding the idea of internal power is vital. Inward power envelops a multi-layered way to deal with mindfulness, integrating components like fearlessness, strength, realness, and reason. The intrinsic strength dwells inside every one of us, ready to be perceived, supported, and released.

Inward power engages us to explore life's difficulties with effortlessness, to seek after our fantasies with relentless assurance, and to live truly lined up with our most profound qualities and wants. It is the establishment whereupon we fabricate an existence of significance, reason, and satisfaction. By diving into the profundities of our being and embracing our internal power, we open the potential for extraordinary development and unlimited conceivable outcomes.

Significance of Self-Revelation

Setting out on the excursion of self-revelation isn't just an extravagance yet a need for driving a satisfying and deliberate life. The significance of digging into the profundities of our being couldn't possibly be more significant, for it is through self-disclosure that we uncover the insights that characterize us and enlighten the way toward our most noteworthy potential.

In a world loaded up with interruptions and outside impacts, it is really quite simple to fail to focus on who we genuinely are and the main thing to us. In any case, by committing time and work to self-reflection and contemplation, we gain important experiences into our interests, values, assets, and desires.

Self-disclosure engages us to pursue cognizant decisions that are lined up with our valid selves, instead of essentially floating through life on autopilot. It empowers us to develop a more profound identity mindfulness and self-acknowledgment, cultivating more prominent strength notwithstanding difficulty and a more significant feeling of satisfaction in our regular routines.

By embracing the excursion of self-revelation, we set out on a groundbreaking way toward living with expectation, reason, and legitimacy. An excursion holds the way to opening our actual potential and releasing the power that exists in every one of us.

Outline of the Excursion Ahead

As we set out on this groundbreaking excursion of self-revelation, acquiring a make comprehension of the way that lies before us is fundamental. In the parts ahead, we will investigate a rich embroidery of bits of knowledge, devices, and practices intended to assist you with uncovering your deepest bits of insight and release your natural influence.

All through this excursion, we will dive into points like figuring out your own qualities, perceiving and beating restricting convictions, embracing legitimacy, developing self-assurance, sustaining internal strength, lining up with your motivation, and showing your fantasies.

Every part will offer a mix of hypothesis, functional activities, and genuine guides to direct you on your mission for mindfulness and strengthening. Whether you are simply starting your excursion of self-revelation or trying to extend how you might interpret yourself, this book fills in as a guide to assist you with exploring the territory of your inward scene with lucidity and reason.

By moving toward this excursion with an open heart and a readiness to investigate the profundities of your being, you will establish the groundwork for a day to day existence loaded up with importance, satisfaction, and unlimited potential. Together, let us set out on this experience of self-revelation and open the power that dwells inside every one of us.

Setting Goals

Before we dive further into the excursion of self-revelation, it is indispensable to set clear goals for what we desire to accomplish and encounter en route. Goals act as our directing stars, giving guidance and concentration as we explore the exciting bends in the road of our inward scene.

Pause for a minute to ponder why you have decided to leave on this excursion. What are your expectations, yearnings, and wants? What do you expect to find out about yourself? How would you imagine your life unfurling as you extend how you might interpret what your identity is?

Setting goals permits us to adjust our activities to our most profound qualities and yearnings, preparing for a more deliberate and satisfying excursion. Whether you will likely develop fearlessness, conquer restricting convictions, or line up with your motivation, articulate it obviously and hold it near your heart as you push ahead.

All through this book, we will return to your goals routinely, involving them as a compass to direct our investigation and keep us secured in our motivation. By setting clear aims and staying open to the conceivable outcomes that unfurl, you will make the space for significant development and change to flourish in your life.

Practices for Reflection

To help you in your excursion of self-revelation, this part offers a choice of activities intended to invigorate thoughtfulness, extend mindfulness, and flash self-awareness. These activities are expected to be more than simple scholarly pursuits; they are solicitations to dig into the profundities of your being and associate with your deepest insights.

Through journaling, contemplation, representation, and other intelligent practices, you will have the potential chance to investigate different features of your character, values, convictions, and goals. These activities are not intended to be finished quickly yet rather relished and investigated at your own speed, permitting bits of knowledge to arise naturally as you draw in with them.

As you set out on these activities, move toward them with a receptive outlook and a readiness to embrace whatever emerges. There are no correct responses; every knowledge, disclosure, and disclosure is a venturing stone on your way to self-revelation.

Keep in mind, self-revelation is an excursion, not an objective. Show restraint toward yourself, and confidence all the while. By devoting time and thoughtfulness regarding these activities, you are moving toward opening the power that exists in you and making a day to day existence that is lined up with your most profound qualities and desires.

| 2 |

Chapter 2: Understanding Self

Investigating Individual Qualities

Leaving on the excursion of self-figuring out starts with a profound investigation of our own qualities — the core values that shape our lives and impact our choices. These qualities act as our sense of direction, guiding us toward what makes the biggest difference to us and giving a system to living legitimately.

To investigate your own qualities, carve out opportunity to consider the standards and beliefs that resound profoundly with you. Consider the times when you have felt generally satisfied, adjusted, and consistent with yourself. What values were available in those minutes? These may incorporate respectability, empathy, innovativeness, trustworthiness, or a feeling of experience, among others.

Whenever you have distinguished your basic beliefs, consider how they as of now manifest in your life. Might it be said that you are residing in arrangement with your qualities, or are there regions where you feel separated or noticeably off? Thinking about these inquiries can give important bits of knowledge into regions to development and potential open doors for more prominent arrangement with your credible self.

Keep in mind, your qualities are one of a kind to you, and there is no correct response. Embrace the course of investigation with interest and receptiveness, permitting yourself to reveal the bits of insight that lie at the core of what your identity is. By getting it and respecting your own qualities, you establish the groundwork for carrying on with a daily existence that is profoundly significant, intentional, and consistent with yourself.

Perceiving Qualities and Shortcomings

In the excursion of self-understanding, developing attention to both our assets and weaknesses is fundamental. Our assets are the characteristics and capacities that engage us to explore life's difficulties with certainty and flexibility, while our shortcomings address regions where we might confront hindrances or constraints.

Find opportunity to think about your assets — those inborn abilities, abilities, and traits that fall into place for you. Think about the exercises or assignments where you succeed and the input you have gotten from others about your assets. Recognize and commend these parts of yourself, perceiving the interesting gifts that you bring to the world.

Simultaneously, recognize your shortcomings — the regions where you might battle or experience hardships. Think about the examples or propensities that might keep you away from arriving at your maximum capacity and consider how you could address or conquer these difficulties.

Recollect that perceiving your shortcomings is certainly not an indication of disappointment yet a chance for development and personal growth. By embracing your shortcomings with sympathy and interest, you can start to foster techniques for conquering them and utilizing your assets to make positive change in your life.

Eventually, by developing consciousness of both your assets and shortcomings, you gain a more profound comprehension of yourself and your extraordinary excursion. Embrace the full range of who you are, realizing that every viewpoint adds to the wealth and intricacy of your experience.

Inspecting Conviction Frameworks

Our conviction frameworks assume a significant part in forming our discernments, ways of behaving, and encounters. They are the focal point through which we view ourselves, others, and our general surroundings, impacting our considerations, feelings, and activities in significant ways. In the excursion of self-understanding, it is fundamental to analyze and comprehend the convictions that underlie our contemplations and ways of behaving.

Start by considering the convictions that you hold about yourself — those profoundly instilled presumptions about your personality, capacities, and worth. Consider where these convictions started, whether they were framed in youth, affected by cultural assumptions, or molded by previous encounters. Are these convictions enabling and strong, or do they restrict your true capacity and keep you away from understanding your fantasies?

Then, investigate your convictions about your general surroundings and individuals in your day to day existence. Consider the presumptions you make about others, the decisions you pass, and the assumptions you hold. Are these convictions in light of proof and experience, or would they say they are shaded by predisposition, bias, or dread?

As you analyze your conviction frameworks, challenge suppositions and question profoundly held convictions that never again serve you. Consider elective viewpoints and search out proof that goes against or challenges your current convictions. Develop an outlook of transparency and interest, perceiving that development and change are intrinsic pieces of the human experience.

By analyzing and understanding your conviction frameworks, you gain knowledge into the basic drivers of your viewpoints, feelings, and ways of behaving. This mindfulness engages you to challenge restricting convictions, embrace enabling viewpoints, and develop a mentality of versatility, plausibility, and development.

Developing Self-Empathy

In our excursion of self-understanding, it is essential to develop an empathetic and supporting relationship with ourselves. Self-sympathy includes broadening a similar graciousness, understanding, and acknowledgment to ourselves that we would propose to a dear companion in the midst of hardship. It is the establishment whereupon we assemble flexibility, fearlessness, and close to home prosperity.

Start by developing familiarity with your internal exchange — the considerations and messages that you routinely direct toward yourself. Notice assuming that your internal pundit will in general be cruel, critical, or unforgiving, and tenderly divert your consideration toward more sympathetic and steady self-talk.

Work on treating yourself with the very graciousness and empathy that you would propose to a friend or family member. Recognize your missteps and deficiencies with understanding and pardoning, perceiving that flaw is a characteristic piece of the human experience. Indulge yourself with the very warmth and care that you would stretch out to a treasured companion, offering uplifting statements, solace, and consolation in the midst of trouble.

Foster ceremonies and practices that support your body, psyche, and soul, like care contemplation, taking care of oneself exercises, and demonstrations of self-articulation and innovativeness. Develop an identity sympathy by participating in exercises that give you pleasure, satisfaction, and a feeling of association with yourself as well as other people.

By developing self-empathy, you establish a supporting inward climate that cultivates flexibility, confidence, and close to home prosperity. You figure out how to explore life's difficulties with beauty and generosity, embracing yourself with genuine love and acknowledgment in each second.

Diary Prompts for Self-Reflection

Participating in ordinary self-reflection through journaling can be an integral asset for extending self-understanding and cultivating self-improvement. Journaling gives a protected and confidential space to investigate your considerations, sentiments, and encounters, permitting you to acquire experiences into your inward world and keep tabs on your development on your excursion of self-revelation.

To start, put away devoted time every day or week to take part in journaling. Find a peaceful and agreeable space where you can reflect without interruptions, and bring a scratch pad or diary and pen to catch your contemplations.

Begin by expounding unreservedly on your encounters, feelings, and perceptions without judgment or oversight. Permit your contemplations to stream normally onto the page, investigating whatever strikes a chord without stressing over punctuation or construction.

You might decide to answer explicit prompts or inquiries to direct your appearance. Consider prompts, for example,

What are my ongoing objectives, goals, and wants?

What are the qualities that are generally critical to me, and how would they impact my choices and activities?

What are the qualities and shortcomings that I have, and how might I use my assets to defeat my shortcomings?

What are the convictions that I hold about myself, others, and my general surroundings, and how would they affect my contemplations, feelings, and ways of behaving?

How might I develop self-empathy and generosity toward myself in snapshots of trouble or challenge?

As you participate in journaling, make sure to move toward the cycle with interest, transparency, and self-sympathy. Permit yourself to investigate your inward world with delicacy and interest, realizing that every reflection carries you more like a more profound comprehension of yourself and your excursion.

By routinely captivating in journaling, you make an act of self-reflection that upholds your development, versatility, and prosperity. You develop your association with yourself and gain important bits of knowledge into your internal world, engaging you to explore life's difficulties with clearness, reason, and credibility.

| 3 |

Chapter 3: Overcoming Limiting Beliefs

Recognizing Restricting Convictions

The most important phase in defeating restricting convictions is to focus a light on the subliminal stories that discreetly impact our considerations, feelings, and activities. These restricting convictions frequently hide underneath the surface, molding our impression of ourselves and our general surroundings in manners that might keep us away from understanding our maximum capacity.

To recognize restricting convictions, start by focusing on repeating designs in your viewpoints and ways of behaving. Notice in the event that there are sure parts of your life where you reliably feel stuck, unfortunate, or lacking. These regions frequently act as pieces of information to the hidden convictions that are influencing everything.

Carve out opportunity to investigate the messages that you incorporated from previous encounters, connections, or cultural molding. Find out if these convictions reflect objective truth or are basically stories that you have acquired or developed over the long run. Challenge suspicions and consider elective points of view that might offer a seriously enabling understanding of the real world.

Journaling can be an important device for revealing restricting convictions, permitting you to investigate your contemplations and sentiments with interest and self-empathy. Expound uninhibitedly on the convictions that you hold about yourself, your capacities, and your true capacity, and notice any repetitive topics or examples that arise.

By focusing a light on your restricting convictions, you venture out toward recovering your power and changing the narratives that shape your life. Embrace this cycle with fortitude and interest, realizing that every knowledge carries you more like a more profound comprehension of yourself and the boundless conceivable outcomes that look for you.

Testing Negative Idea Examples

Whenever you've distinguished the restricting convictions that are keeping you down, the following stage is to stand up to the negative idea designs that propagate them. Negative idea examples can appear as self-question, feeling of dread toward disappointment, or a steady inward pundit that subverts your certainty and confidence.

To challenge negative idea designs, begin by developing consciousness of your viewpoints as they emerge. Notice while you're participating in self-basic or pessimist thinking, and tenderly divert your consideration toward more sure and enabling viewpoints.

Work on reexamining negative contemplations into additional decent and helpful stories. Rather than review misfortunes as proof of individual disappointment, think about them as any open doors for development and learning. Challenge the legitimacy of your negative convictions by looking for proof in actuality and taking into account elective translations of the real world.

Foster a collection of positive confirmations and self-converse with check negative idea designs. Confirmations are strong articulations that state positive bits of insight about yourself and your abilities, serving to reinvent your psyche mind and build up enabling convictions.

Take part in exercises that advance care and mindfulness, like contemplation, yoga, or profound breathing activities. These practices can assist you with developing a more prominent feeling of presence and viewpoint, empowering you to notice your contemplations without becoming ensnared in them.

By testing negative idea designs, you disturb the pattern of self-restriction and make space for additional opportunities to arise. Embrace this cycle with persistence and perseverance, knowing that every little change in context carries you more like an existence of more prominent opportunity, satisfaction, and legitimacy.

Procedures for Reexamining Convictions

Refraiming convictions is an extraordinary interaction that includes moving from an outlook of constraint to one of strengthening. It expects us to look at our convictions through another focal point, one that perceives the innate potential inside us and the conceivable outcomes that exist past our apparent constraints.

One strong strategy for reevaluating convictions is mental rebuilding, which includes recognizing and testing the hidden suspicions that fuel our restricting convictions. By scrutinizing the legitimacy of these suppositions and investigating elective viewpoints, we can start to destroy the establishments whereupon our restricting convictions are assembled.

Another viable strategy is mental social treatment (CBT), which includes methodicallly supplanting negative idea designs with additional positive and versatile ones. Through activities like idea checking, mental rebuilding, and conduct tests, CBT assists us with growing better approaches for thinking and acting that are more lined up with our objectives and values.

Representation is one more powerful apparatus for reevaluating convictions, as it permits us to practice new situations and results that challenge our restricting convictions intellectually. By distinctively envisioning ourselves succeeding, we can start to reinvent our psyche mind and develop a more noteworthy feeling of certainty and self-viability.

At last, rehearsing self-empathy and self-acknowledgment is fundamental for reevaluating convictions, as it permits us to move toward ourselves and our encounters with graciousness and understanding. By treating ourselves with sympathy, we can start to challenge the cruel self-decisions and reactions that build up our restricting convictions, preparing for a more certain and enabling mentality.

As you investigate these procedures for reevaluating convictions, recall that change takes time and tolerance. Be delicate with yourself as you explore this interaction, and commend every little triumph en route. By embracing the excursion of self-disclosure and strengthening, you free yourself up to a universe of boundless conceivable outcomes and potential.

Insistences and Representation

Insistences and representation are amazing assets for reconstructing the psyche mind and supporting positive convictions. Attestations are positive explanations that affirm the characteristics, capacities, and results we want in our lives. By rehashing insistences routinely, we can overwrite negative self-talk and ingrain new, enabling convictions.

While creating assertions, it's crucial for use language that is positive, current state, and by and by significant. Rather than saying, "I will be certain," avow, "I'm sure and competent in each circumstance." Rehash your confirmations everyday, in a perfect world in the first part of the day or before bed, to insert them profoundly into your psyche mind.

Perception supplements certifications by connecting with the creative mind to make striking mental pictures of wanted results. By picturing ourselves accomplishing our objectives and encapsulating our ideal selves, we enact similar brain processes in the mind as though we were really encountering those occasions.

To rehearse representation, find a tranquil space where you won't be upset and shut your eyes. Envision yourself succeeding, feeling sure, and typifying the characteristics you want. Connect every one of your faculties to make the perception as genuine and vivid as could be expected. Picture yourself beating difficulties effortlessly, achieving your objectives, and carrying on with the existence of your fantasies.

Consolidating confirmations with representation makes a strong cooperative energy that intensifies their viability. By reliably rehearsing these strategies, you can revamp your mind to line up with your most elevated yearnings and open your maximum capacity. Embrace the force of confirmations and perception as instruments for changing your convictions and making the existence you genuinely want.

Contextual investigations and Examples of overcoming adversity

Drawing motivation from genuine models can be significantly inspiring and enlightening on our excursion to conquer restricting convictions. Contextual investigations and examples of overcoming adversity give substantial proof that change is conceivable and offer important experiences into the procedures and outlook moves that lead to leap forwards.

Investigate contextual analyses of people who have effectively beaten their restricting convictions and accomplished momentous self-awareness. Focus on the particular difficulties they confronted, the convictions they held, and the means they took to break liberated from purposeful restrictions. Observe the methodologies, procedures, and attitude moves that were instrumental in their prosperity.

Moreover, drench yourself in examples of overcoming adversity that reverberate with your own encounters and yearnings. These accounts act as strong updates that you are in good company in your battles and that others have confronted comparative snags and arisen more grounded and stronger. Permit yourself to be propelled by their excursions and utilize their triumphs as fuel for your own change.

As you investigate contextual analyses and examples of overcoming adversity, consider how their encounters connect with your own life and difficulties. Consider how you can apply the illustrations learned and the systems utilized to your own excursion of conquering restricting convictions. Draw strength from their victories and let their accounts act as encouraging signs and probability on your way to strengthening.

By concentrating on contextual investigations and examples of overcoming adversity, you extend your consciousness of what is conceivable and gain significant bits of knowledge into the mentality movements and procedures that lead to individual change. Allow these accounts to move and engage you as you explore your own excursion of beating restricting convictions and venturing into your fullest potential.

| 4 |

Chapter 4: Embracing Authenticity

Embracing Weakness

At the core of realness lies weakness, the fortitude to appear as our actual selves, flaws what not. Embracing weakness is definitely not an indication of shortcoming yet a significant demonstration of solidarity and validness. It expects us to recognize and embrace our feelings of trepidation, frailties, and vulnerabilities, and to permit ourselves to be seen and known completely.

Weakness makes the way for bona fide associations and significant connections, as it welcomes others to meet us with sympathy, empathy, and acknowledgment. At the point when we permit ourselves to be defenseless, we make space for authentic closeness and association with thrive, liberated from the imperatives of affectation or hairsplitting.

To embrace weakness, begin by recognizing and tolerating your own blemishes and weaknesses without judgment or self-analysis. Perceive that weakness is a characteristic and fundamental piece of the human experience, and that by embracing it, you free yourself up to more profound degrees of genuineness and association.

Work on sharing your contemplations, sentiments, and encounters genuinely with others, regardless of whether it feels awkward or frightening from the start. Make dangers and stride beyond your usual range of familiarity, realizing that weakness is the doorway to development, closeness, and genuine having a place.

By embracing weakness, you recover your power and realness, and welcome others to do likewise. Embrace the excellence and wealth of your flaws, and permit yourself to be recognized the truth about and known. In weakness, you will track down the boldness to live really and earnestly, and to manufacture certifiable associations that support and support you on your excursion.

Respecting Individual Bits of insight

Genuineness prospers when we honor our own bits of insight and live in arrangement with our most profound qualities and convictions. Our own insights are the core values that illuminate our considerations, choices, and activities, forming the course of our lives and characterizing who we are at our center.

To respect your own insights, begin by finding opportunity to consider the main thing to you and what presents to you a feeling of satisfaction and reason. Consider the qualities and convictions that reverberate most profoundly with you, and distinguish the rules that you hold dear to your heart.

Whenever you have recognized your own bits of insight, endeavor to live in arrangement with them in all parts of your life. Decide and choices that mirror your qualities and needs, in any event, when confronted with difficulties or resistance. Trust in your instinct and inward insight to direct you on the way that is consistent with yourself.

Practice genuineness by offering your viewpoints, sentiments, and assessments sincerely and straightforwardly, regardless of whether they contrast from those of others. Stand firm in your convictions and talk your reality with boldness and trustworthiness, realizing that credibility is a strong power for association and change.

As you honor your own bits of insight and live really, you make a daily existence that is wealthy in importance, reason, and satisfaction. You develop a profound identity regard and self-strengthening, and motivate others to do likewise. Embrace the force of realness by respecting your own bits of insight and living in arrangement with your most profound qualities and convictions.

Relinquishing Endorsement Looking for Ways of behaving

One of the best hindrances to credibility is the steady quest for outside approval and endorsement. At the point when we look for approval from others, we surrender our power and organization, permitting the suppositions and assumptions for others to direct our contemplations, ways of behaving, and identity worth.

To develop genuineness, it is fundamental to perceive and deliver endorsement looking for ways of behaving that sabotage our certainty and independence. Start by thinking about the manners by which you look for approval from others, whether through looking for endorsement, commendation, or approval of your decisions and activities.

Notice what these endorsement looking for ways of behaving mean for your viewpoints, feelings, and ways of behaving. Do you wind up undermining your qualities or forfeiting your realness to acquire acknowledgment or endorsement from others? Could it be said that you are continually looking for consolation or approval from outer sources to feel commendable or esteemed?

Whenever you have recognized endorsement looking for ways of behaving, challenge them with mindfulness and self-sympathy. Perceive that looking for approval from others is a characteristic human inclination, however at last a vain pursuit just subverts your healthy identity worth and credibility.

All things being equal, center around developing self-endorsement and self-approval from the inside. Perceive your intrinsic worth and worth as a novel individual, free of the feelings or decisions of others. Trust in your own instinct and internal insight to direct you on the way that is consistent with yourself, paying little mind to outer approval or endorsement.

Work on stating your limits and talking your reality with certainty and conviction, regardless of whether it implies taking a chance with objection or dismissal from others. Recall that genuineness requires fortitude and weakness, and that genuine association and having a place must be found when we embrace our true selves completely and proudly.

By relinquishing endorsement looking for ways of behaving and embracing self-endorsement and approval, you recover your power and organization, and step into the totality of your legitimacy. Embrace the opportunity and strengthening that comes from living legitimately, and trust in the worth of your own novel voice and point of view.

Developing Bona fide Associations

Legitimacy flourishes in the dirt of authentic associations — connections established on shared regard, understanding, and acknowledgment. Developing valid associations expects us to appear as our actual selves, helpless and flawed, and to welcome others to do likewise.

To develop valid associations, begin by being legitimate and straightforward in your communications with others. Share your considerations, sentiments, and encounters straightforwardly and truly, unafraid of judgment or dismissal. Permit yourself to be perceived the truth about and known, imperfections and all, and expand a similar acknowledgment and understanding to other people.

Practice undivided attention and compassion in your connections, trying to grasp others' points of view and encounters without judgment or preventiveness. Make a protected and steady space for others to articulate their thoughts legitimately, liberated from the strain to adjust or perform.

Embrace weakness and closeness in your connections, realizing that genuine association expects us to let down our walls and permit others to see us as we are. Share your delights, distresses, expectations, and fears with those you trust, and be available to help and elevate them consequently.

Pick connections that support and inspire you, encircling yourself with individuals who honor and praise your legitimacy and urge you to be the best version of yourself. Relinquish connections that request you to forfeit your validness or undermine your qualities, realizing that genuine association can flourish in a climate of shared regard and acknowledgment.

By developing credible associations, you make an organization of help and having a place that improves your life and supports you on your excursion of self-disclosure and development. Embrace the influence of valid associations with sustain your spirit, elevate your soul, and improve your life in manners that are unimaginable.

Self-Articulation Activities

Participating in self-articulation activities can be a strong method for extending your association with your genuine self and develop a more prominent feeling of legitimacy in your life. These activities give an innovative outlet to investigating and offering your viewpoints, feelings, and encounters, permitting you to interface with yourself on a more profound level and impart your reality to the world.

One successful self-articulation practice is journaling, which gives a protected and confidential space to investigate your contemplations, sentiments, and encounters without judgment or restraint. Put away opportunity every day to expound openly on whatever is at the forefront of your thoughts, permitting your considerations to stream onto the page without blue penciling or altering yourself. Journaling can assist you with acquiring clearness, process feelings, and reveal bits of knowledge into your inward world.

One more impressive self-articulation practice is imaginative articulation through workmanship, music, or development. Participate in exercises that permit you to communicate your thoughts imaginatively, whether it's painting, drawing, playing an instrument, moving, or singing. Permit yourself to take advantage of your inward inventiveness and articulate your thoughts genuinely through your picked medium.

You can likewise take part in self-articulation practices through discussion and exchange with confided in companions, relatives, or specialists. Share your contemplations, sentiments, and encounters straightforwardly and truly, and listen profoundly to others as they do likewise. Credible correspondence cultivates association and understanding, permitting you to put yourself out there legitimately and be seen and heard by others.

Anything self-articulation practices you decide to take part in, move toward them with receptiveness, interest, and self-empathy. Permit yourself to investigate and explore different avenues regarding various types of articulation, and confidence in your instinct to direct you toward exercises that resound with your valid self.

By taking part in self-articulation practices consistently, you can extend your association with your real self and develop a more prominent feeling of validness in your life. Embrace the force of self-articulation to convey your reality, interface with others, and carry on with a daily existence that is consistent with yourself.

| **5** |

Chapter 5: Cultivating Self-Confidence

Figuring out the Idea of Fearlessness

Self-assurance, frequently viewed as the foundation of individual strengthening, is a multi-layered property that incorporates convictions, mentalities, and ways of behaving. It appears as a profound identity confirmation and confidence in one's capacities, permitting people to explore life's difficulties with flexibility, emphaticness, and elegance.

To develop self-assurance, it's vital for first grasp its inclination and parts. Self-assurance isn't simply a perspective however a unique exchange of variables that shape our impression of ourselves and our capacities. These variables incorporate self-adequacy, which alludes to our faith in our capacity to accomplish explicit objectives and undertakings; confidence, which envelops our general identity worth and worth; and mental self portrait, which reflects how we see ourselves and our position on the planet.

Self-assurance is additionally impacted by outer variables, like previous encounters, criticism from others, and the social and social setting where we work. Positive encounters of progress and approval can support fearlessness, while misfortunes and analysis can sabotage it.

By understanding the idea of self-assurance, we gain knowledge into the wellsprings of our own certainty and regions where we might have to develop more prominent confidence in ourselves. We perceive that self-assurance isn't fixed or unchanging yet can be supported and created through purposeful exertion and practice.

As we set out on the excursion of developing fearlessness, let us embrace the force of mindfulness and self-reflection to extend how we might interpret ourselves and our abilities. Allow us to perceive the intrinsic worth and potential inside us and focus on supporting a mentality of confidence and faith in our capacity to conquer obstructions and accomplish our objectives. In doing as such, we make ready for a day to day existence loaded up with certainty, versatility, and limitless potential.

Beating Self-Uncertainty

One of the most considerable obstructions to fearlessness is self-question — the irritating voice of vulnerability and dread that murmurs, "You're not adequate" or "You won't ever succeed." Left uncontrolled, self-uncertainty can dissolve our certainty, sabotage our endeavors, and keep us away from understanding our maximum capacity.

To develop fearlessness, it is fundamental to face and defeat self-question head-on. This starts with creating consciousness of the contemplations and convictions that fuel self-question and remembering them as simple discernments, instead of changeless bits of insight.

Challenge self-uncertainty by scrutinizing its legitimacy and looking for proof running against the norm. Ask yourself, "What proof do I need to help this conviction?" and "Have I prevailed in comparable circumstances previously?" Frequently, you'll observe that self-question depends on unwarranted presumptions or misshaped view of the real world.

Supplant self-uncertainty with attestations of self-conviction and strengthening. Certifications are strong explanations that state positive bits of insight about yourself and your abilities. Rehash confirmations, for example, "I'm competent," "I put stock in myself," and "I confide in my capacities" routinely to reinvent your psyche mind and build up an outlook of self-assurance.

Practice self-empathy and self-acknowledgment even with self-question. Indulge yourself with graciousness and understanding, perceiving that self-question is a characteristic piece of the human experience and doesn't characterize your value or potential. Embrace blemish and disappointment as any open doors for development and learning, instead of proof of insufficiency.

At long last, make a move in spite of self-question. Boldness isn't the shortfall of dread yet the eagerness to act despite it. Propel yourself outside your usual range of familiarity, proceed with carefully thought out plans of action, and praise your victories — regardless of how little. With each step in the right direction, you'll gather speed and trust in your capacity to conquer self-question and accomplish your objectives.

By facing and beating self-question, you recover your power and organization, and develop an outlook of fearlessness and confidence. Embrace the excursion of self-revelation and development, knowing that with tirelessness and assurance, you can beat any obstruction and understand your fullest potential.

Building Skill and Dominance

A critical driver of fearlessness is capability — the confidence in one's capacity to perform successfully in unambiguous regions or undertakings. Building capability requires commitment, practice, and an eagerness to push past one's usual range of familiarity in quest for dominance.

To develop self-assurance through capability, begin by distinguishing areas of interest or energy where you might want to foster your abilities and skill. Whether it's learning another dialect, dominating an instrument, or leveling up your initiative skills, pick exercises that reverberate with your qualities and goals.

Set explicit, attainable objectives that challenge you to extend past your ongoing abilities. Separate bigger objectives into more modest, sensible advances, and make an arrangement for how you will accomplish them. Praise your advancement en route, and perceive every little triumph as proof of your developing ability.

Drench yourself in learning and work on, devoting time and work to leveling up your abilities and growing your insight. Embrace the course of experimentation, perceiving that mishaps and disappointments are inescapable pieces of the learning venture. Move toward difficulties with versatility and assurance, realizing that every snag you beat carries you one bit nearer to dominance.

Search out open doors for input and development, whether through proper preparation projects, mentorship, or helpful analysis from peers. Use criticism as an instrument for learning and improvement, and be available to consolidating ideas for how you can upgrade your presentation.

As you fabricate skill and dominance in your picked regions, you'll see a relating expansion in self-assurance. Trust in your capacities and put stock in your ability to succeed, realizing that the abilities and information you've gained have prepared you to confront any test with certainty and flexibility. By putting resources into your turn of events and embracing the excursion of dominance, you establish the groundwork for a day to day existence loaded up with confidence and accomplishment.

Tackling Positive Self-Talk

The manner in which we address ourselves significantly affects our fearlessness and generally prosperity. Positive self-talk includes developing a steady and empowering inward exchange that inspires and enables us, instead of destroying us with analysis and self-question.

To outfit the force of positive self-talk, begin by becoming mindful of the contemplations and convictions that overwhelm your internal discourse. Notice assuming that your self-talk will in general be negative or self-basic, and challenge those examples with sympathy and mindfulness.

Supplant negative self-talk with attestations and positive explanations that assert your value, capacities, and potential. Pick states that impact you by and by and mirror the characteristics and values you try to exemplify. Rehash these insistences routinely, both verbally and intellectually, to reinvent your psyche mind and support an outlook of fearlessness and self-conviction.

Work on reexamining negative considerations into more helpful and enabling points of view. Rather than harping on past disappointments or saw deficiencies, center around the illustrations learned and the headway made. Develop appreciation for your assets and accomplishments, regardless of how little, and recognize your strength and assurance notwithstanding challenges.

Encircle yourself with energy and motivation by searching out steady impacts and conditions. Encircle yourself with individuals who elevate and empower you, and participate in exercises that give you pleasure and satisfaction. Establish a supporting internal climate that cultivates self-sympathy, self-acknowledgment, and self esteem.

By bridling the force of positive self-talk, you develop an outlook of fearlessness and confidence that enables you to explore life's difficulties with beauty and flexibility. Embrace the act of addressing yourself with thoughtfulness, consolation, and confidence in your intrinsic worth and potential. In doing as such, you'll open the boundless potential inside you and step into a day to day existence loaded up with certainty, reason, and satisfaction.

Venturing Outside Safe places

Genuine development and self-assurance frequently lie just past the limits of our usual ranges of familiarity. Venturing outside our usual ranges of familiarity includes embracing distress and vulnerability in quest for self-awareness, learning, and self-disclosure. While it might feel overwhelming from the outset, wandering into an unknown area offers important open doors for extension and change.

To develop self-assurance through venturing outside safe places, begin by distinguishing regions where you feel stuck or stale in your life. These might be circumstances where dread or self-question keeps you away from making a move or seeking after your objectives. Perceive that inconvenience is a characteristic piece of the development interaction and a sign that you are extending past your ongoing limits.

Put forth unambiguous objectives that challenge you to push past your usual range of familiarity and grow your viewpoints. Separate bigger objectives into more modest, reasonable advances, and focus on making a predictable move toward their accomplishment. Embrace the outlook of trial and error and investigation, realizing that disappointment isn't a misfortune however a chance for learning and development.

Practice self-empathy and self-acknowledgment as you explore outside your usual range of familiarity. Be delicate with yourself and recognize that uneasiness is a typical reaction to new circumstances. Commend your mental fortitude and strength in venturing outside your usual range of familiarity, no matter what the result.

Search out help and support from others as you adventure into a new area. Encircle yourself with individuals who have confidence in your true capacity and urge you to seek after your fantasies. Draw motivation from their accounts of development and change, realizing that you are in good company on your excursion.

By reliably venturing outside your usual range of familiarity, you extend your ability for fearlessness and versatility. You foster a more prominent feeling of confidence in yourself and your capacities, and develop the boldness to confront life's difficulties with elegance and assurance. Embrace the excursion of development and self-disclosure, realizing that each step outside your usual range of familiarity carries you closer to understanding your fullest potential and carrying on with an existence of direction and satisfaction.

| 6 |

Chapter 6: Nurturing Inner Strength

Developing Strength

Versatility, frequently portrayed as the capacity to quickly return from difficulty, is a basic part of internal strength. It is the ability to endure and explore life's difficulties, mishaps, and difficulties with elegance, mental fortitude, and steadiness. Developing flexibility is fundamental for flourishing notwithstanding misfortune and tackling the influence of difficulty as an impetus for development and change.

To develop versatility, it's essential to take on a development outlook — a faith in your capacity to learn, develop, and adjust because of difficulties. Move toward affliction as a chance for development and learning, instead of as an impossible snag. Perceive that difficulties and disappointments are not characteristic of your value or potential but rather are just essential for the excursion toward progress and satisfaction.

Foster mindfulness and the ability to appreciate anyone on a deeper level to all the more likely figure out your responses and reactions to misfortune. Practice care and self-reflection to notice your contemplations, feelings, and ways of behaving without judgment or connection.

Develop a feeling of viewpoint and strength by zeroing in on the things inside your control and relinquishing what you can't change.

Fabricate areas of strength for an organization of companions, family, and coaches who can give direction, support, and point of view during testing times. Encircle yourself with individuals who elevate and motivate you, and rest on them for help when required. Develop connections that depend on trust, compassion, and common regard, and give backing to others as a trade off.

Practice taking care of oneself and self-empathy to sustain your physical, close to home, and mental prosperity. Focus on exercises that sustain and renew your energy, like activity, reflection, side interests, and investing time in nature. Be caring and humane toward yourself, particularly during seasons of trouble or battle, and recognize your assets and strength notwithstanding misfortune.

By developing flexibility, you foster a profound well of inward strength that empowers you to explore life's difficulties with boldness, elegance, and versatility. Embrace affliction as a chance for development and change, and confidence in your capacity to beat any snag that comes your direction. In doing as such, you open the force of strength to flourish despite difficulty and make an existence of importance, reason, and satisfaction.

Rehearsing Self-Sympathy

Self-sympathy is a foundation of internal strength and close to home prosperity. It includes treating oneself with benevolence, understanding, and acknowledgment, particularly during seasons of trouble, disappointment, or languishing. Developing self-sympathy permits us to explore life's difficulties with more prominent versatility, mindfulness, and close to home equilibrium.

To rehearse self-sympathy, begin by recognizing and approving your own encounters and feelings without judgment or analysis. Perceive that it is typical to encounter troublesome feelings like bitterness, dread, or disappointment, and proposition yourself the very sympathy and understanding that you would to a dear companion in comparable conditions.

Practice taking care of oneself by focusing on exercises that feed and recharge your physical, profound, and mental prosperity. Take part in exercises that give you pleasure, unwinding, and satisfaction, whether it's investing energy with friends and family, chasing after leisure activities, or rehearsing care and reflection. Indulge yourself with generosity and delicacy, and pay attention to your body's necessities with sympathy and mindfulness.

Challenge your inward pundit and negative self-talk with self-merciful reactions. At the point when you notice yourself taking part in self-basic or self-accusing considerations, tenderly divert your consideration toward additional humane and grasping viewpoints. Advise yourself that you are human, and that blemish and slip-ups are an unavoidable piece of the human experience.

Develop a feeling of viewpoint and care by recognizing the normal humankind of torment. Perceive that you are in good company to encounter difficulties or mishaps, and that all people share in the delights and distresses of life. Associate with other people who can offer sympathy, backing, and understanding, and give equivalent to a trade off.

By rehearsing self-empathy, you support a profound feeling of internal strength and versatility that permits you to explore life's difficulties effortlessly and elegance. Embrace yourself with graciousness and understanding, and develop a relationship with yourself in light of adoration, acknowledgment, and empathy. In doing as such, you open the force of self-sympathy to encourage close to home prosperity and develop inward strength even with misfortune.

Developing Care

Care is a strong practice for sustaining internal strength and upgrading generally prosperity. It includes giving conscious consideration to the current second with transparency, interest, and acknowledgment, without judgment or connection. Developing care permits us to foster more noteworthy mindfulness, close to home guideline, and strength despite life's difficulties.

To develop care, start by carrying attention to your breath and substantial sensations. Take a couple of seconds to delay and tune into the vibes of your breath as it moves all through your body. Notice the ascent and fall of your chest, the impression of air going through your noses, and the sensation of your body upheld by the ground underneath you.

Practice careful attention to your viewpoints and feelings by noticing them with interest and nonjudgmental mindfulness. Notice the contemplations that emerge to you without becoming involved with them or attempting to change them. Also, notice your feelings surprisingly go, permitting them to move through you without obstruction or connection.

Participate in everyday care rehearses, like reflection, yoga, or careful strolling, to develop a more prominent feeling of presence and mindfulness in your day to day existence. Put away committed time every day to participate in these practices, regardless of whether it's only for a couple of moments, and notice what they mean for your general feeling of prosperity and internal strength.

Integrate care into your day to day exercises by carrying careful attention to basic undertakings like eating, strolling, or washing dishes. Notice the sensations, sights, sounds, and scents related with these exercises, and carry your complete focus to the current second.

By developing care, you foster a more noteworthy ability to answer life's difficulties with lucidity, poise, and flexibility. Embrace the act of care as an integral asset for sustaining internal strength and upgrading by and large prosperity, and permit it to direct you on the way toward more prominent mindfulness, equilibrium, and satisfaction.

Defining Limits

Defining limits is fundamental for supporting internal strength and safeguarding your profound prosperity. Limits characterize the constraints of satisfactory way of behaving and communications, permitting you to keep a feeling of independence, sense of pride, and individual honesty in your connections and collaborations with others.

To develop internal strength through defining limits, begin by distinguishing your own requirements, values, and cutoff points. Ponder what is vital to you and what ways of behaving or connections are unsuitable or hurtful. Trust yourself to respect and focus on your own prosperity, regardless of whether it implies defining limits that others may not comprehend or concur with.

Impart your limits plainly, decisively, and deferentially with others. Use "I" proclamations to communicate your necessities and inclinations, and put forth firm yet merciful lines on conduct that crosses your limits. Implement your limits reliably and without conciliatory sentiment, regardless of whether it implies disheartening or disturbing others.

Practice taking care of oneself and self-sympathy as you explore the most common way of defining limits. Perceive that it is normal to feel remorseful or restless about attesting your limits, particularly assuming you are acquainted with focusing on others' necessities over your own. Advise yourself that defining limits is a demonstration of taking care of oneself and self confidence, and that you have the right to focus on your own prosperity.

Be ready to uphold ramifications for limit infringement, whether it's eliminating yourself from a circumstance, finishing a discussion, or moving away from people who reliably ignore your limits. Trust in your own judgment and instinct to direct you in deciding when and how to really uphold your limits.

By defining limits, you make a defensive safeguard around your profound prosperity and develop a more prominent feeling of inward strength, sense of pride, and strengthening. Embrace the act of defining limits as an amazing asset for supporting your psychological, profound, and otherworldly wellbeing, and confidence in your capacity to respect and focus on your own necessities and limits with certainty and elegance.

Embracing Development Mentality

Embracing a development mentality is a strong method for sustaining inward strength and flexibility. A development mentality includes having faith in your ability to learn, develop, and adjust in light of difficulties, misfortunes, and disappointments. It is described by a faith in the force of exertion, determination, and gaining from botches as fundamental elements for progress and self-improvement.

To develop a development outlook, begin by reexamining difficulties and misfortunes as any open doors for development and learning. Rather than survey snags as impossible obstructions or indications of disappointment, consider them to be important chances to foster new abilities, bits of knowledge, and techniques for progress.

Work on embracing a "yet" outlook, perceiving that you might not have dominated an expertise or accomplished an objective "yet," yet that with time, exertion, and persistence, you can and will gain ground. Move toward difficulties with interest, transparency, and an eagerness to try and investigate additional opportunities.

Praise your endeavors and progress, regardless of how little, and recognize the flexibility and assurance it takes to seek after development and learning despite affliction. Perceive that difficulties and disappointments are not marks of your value or potential but rather are essentially important for the excursion toward progress and satisfaction.

Develop self-empathy and self-acknowledgment as you explore the high points and low points of the development interaction. Indulge yourself with consideration and understanding, particularly during seasons of trouble or battle, and recognize your endeavors and progress with satisfaction and appreciation.

By embracing a development outlook, you encourage a more prominent feeling of internal strength, flexibility, and confidence. You foster the certainty and versatility to confront life's difficulties with boldness and assurance, realizing that each mishap is a chance for development and each disappointment is a venturing stone on the way to progress. Embrace the excursion of development and learning, and confidence in your capacity to beat snags and accomplish your objectives with effortlessness and strength.

| 7 |

Chapter 7: Aligning with Purpose

Finding Your Energy

Finding your energy is a critical stage in lining up with your motivation. Enthusiasm is the fuel that lights your inward fire, driving you toward exercises, pursuits, and tries that give you pleasure, satisfaction, and a feeling of significance. To find your energy, leave on an excursion of self-investigation and interest, permitting yourself to investigate a large number of interests and exercises without judgment or strain.

Begin by pondering minutes in your day to day existence when you felt generally alive, drew in, and empowered. Think about exercises or leisure activities that you normally incline toward, regardless of whether you haven't sought after them in some time. Focus on the things that give you pleasure, energy, and a feeling of stream, where time appears to stop as you submerge yourself completely in the experience.

Explore different avenues regarding new exercises and encounters to grow your points of view and uncover stowed away interests. Step outside your usual range of familiarity and attempt things you've never finished, whether it's mastering another expertise, investigating another side interest, or chipping in for a purpose that impacts you. Be available to surprising disclosures and open doors that might emerge en route.

Stand by listening to your instinct and internal direction as you investigate various ways and conceivable outcomes. Notice the sensations of energy, interest, and excitement that emerge when you participate in exercises that line up with your interests and interests. Trust yourself to understand what feels right and significant for you, and rely on your instinct's calling any place it might lead.

Embrace the course of self-revelation with persistence, interest, and self-sympathy. Know that finding your enthusiasm is an excursion of investigation and trial and error, and that it's OK to attempt various things and head in a different direction en route. Remain open to new encounters and amazing open doors, and trust that the way to finding your enthusiasm will unfurl time permitting and in its own extraordinary manner.

By finding your enthusiasm, you open the way to lining up with your motivation and carrying on with a daily existence loaded up with significance, satisfaction, and bliss. Embrace the excursion of self-revelation with boldness and interest, realizing that the quest for enthusiasm is a strong impetus for self-awareness, change, and carrying on with a day to day existence that genuinely resounds with your entire being.

Explaining Your Qualities

Explaining your qualities is fundamental for lining up with your motivation and carrying on with a daily existence that is genuine, significant, and satisfying. Values are the core values that characterize what is generally vital to you and illuminate your choices, activities, and needs. At the point when your activities are in arrangement with your qualities, you experience a more prominent feeling of realness, satisfaction, and inward congruity.

To explain your qualities, find opportunity to think about what makes the biggest difference to you throughout everyday life. Consider the characteristics and attributes that you respect and try to typify, both in yourself and in others. Ponder minutes in your day to day existence when you felt generally alive, satisfied, and lined up with your actual self, and distinguish the qualities that were available in those encounters.

Make a rundown of your guiding principle, positioning them arranged by significance to you. Consider values like trustworthiness, genuineness, empathy, mental fortitude, inventiveness, development, and commitment to other people. Be straightforward with yourself about what really impacts you and what feels generally legitimate and significant for you actually.

Consider how your qualities line up with various aspects of your life, including your connections, vocation, wellbeing, and self-awareness. Notice any regions where there might be inconsistencies between your qualities and your activities, and investigate ways of carrying more noteworthy arrangement and honesty to those areas.

Utilize your qualities as a compass to direct your choices, activities, and needs throughout everyday life. When confronted with decisions or difficulties, ask yourself, "Does this line up with my qualities?" and let your qualities act as a guidepost for settling on choices that are in arrangement with your actual self.

By explaining your qualities, you make a guide for carrying on with a daily existence that is true, significant, and lined up with your motivation. Embrace your qualities as core values for exploring life's excursion with respectability, genuineness, and inward congruity, and trust that when you honor your qualities, you make a day to day existence that mirrors the genuine substance of what your identity is and a big motivator for you.

Laying out Significant Objectives

Laying out significant objectives is a critical stage in lining up with your motivation and making an existence of satisfaction and reason. Objectives give an internal compass and concentration, directing your activities and decisions toward the acknowledgment of your fantasies and yearnings. At the point when your objectives are lined up with your interests, values, and reason, they become strong impetuses for development, change, and individual satisfaction.

To lay out significant objectives, start by explaining your vision for the future and recognizing what you need to accomplish in various parts of your life. Think about your interests, interests, and values, and contemplate how you can adjust your objectives to these center parts of yourself. Envision the sort of life you need to make for you and envision what it might look and feel want to accomplish your most treasured dreams and desires.

Separate your drawn out vision into more modest, significant objectives that are explicit, quantifiable, attainable, pertinent, and time-bound (Brilliant). Every objective ought to be clear, concrete, and feasible, with a characterized course of events and achievements for following advancement. By separating your objectives into more modest advances, you make them more reasonable and improve your probability of achievement.

Focus on your objectives in view of their significance and pertinence to your general vision and values. Center around the objectives that are generally lined up with your interests, values, and reason, and allot your time, energy, and assets appropriately. Relinquish objectives that never again impact you or line up with your ongoing needs, and be available to changing your objectives depending on the situation in light of changing conditions or new experiences.

Make a strategy for accomplishing your objectives, framing the particular advances, assets, and backing you should make them a reality. Separate your arrangement into noteworthy assignments and timetable them into your schedule to guarantee reliable advancement and responsibility. Commend your victories en route, regardless of how little, and use them as fuel to move you toward your next achievement.

By defining significant objectives that are lined up with your interests, values, and reason, you make a guide for carrying on with an existence of satisfaction, reason, and importance. Embrace the excursion of objective setting as a chance for development, self-disclosure, and strengthening, and confidence in your capacity to accomplish your fantasies and goals with commitment, diligence, and flexibility.

Embracing Difficulties as Learning experiences

Embracing difficulties as learning experiences is fundamental for lining up with your motivation and understanding your fullest potential. Challenges are an unavoidable piece of life, yet they likewise offer significant open doors for learning, advancement, and self-revelation. At the point when you approach difficulties with a development mentality, you develop versatility, flexibility, and fortitude, enabling you to defeat hindrances and flourish despite misfortune.

To embrace difficulties as learning experiences, shift your viewpoint from review them as snags to amazing open doors for learning and personal growth. Rather than seeing difficulties as dangers to your prosperity or achievement, view them as solicitations to extend past your usual range of familiarity, grow your capacities, and find new qualities and capacities inside yourself.

Work on reevaluating negative convictions and suspicions about challenges into seriously engaging and hopeful viewpoints. Rather than harping on the potential for disappointment or difficulty, center around the potential for development, learning, and self-disclosure that difficulties offer. Trust in your capacity to explore difficulties with effortlessness and flexibility, realizing that each deterrent you defeat carries you one bit nearer to understanding your objectives and goals.

Embrace vulnerability and inconvenience as regular parts of the development cycle, and incline toward them with boldness and interest. Perceive that development and change frequently happen outside your usual range of familiarity, and embrace the obscure and investigate additional opportunities. Move toward difficulties with a feeling of receptiveness and adaptability, realizing that every hindrance you face presents a chance for development and self-revelation.

Search out help and direction from tutors, mentors, or believed loved ones as you explore difficulties and mishaps. Draw strength from their insight, consolation, and viewpoint, and rest on them for direction and backing when required. Recall that you are in good company on your excursion, and that others have confronted comparable difficulties and arisen more grounded and stronger accordingly.

By embracing difficulties as learning experiences, you develop a mentality of flexibility, versatility, and fortitude that enables you to defeat hindrances and flourish notwithstanding misfortune. Embrace the excursion of development and self-revelation with an open heart and an eagerness to gain and develop from each insight, realizing that difficulties are not misfortunes but rather venturing stones on the way to understanding your fullest potential.

Developing an Intentional Outlook

Developing a deliberate mentality is vital to lining up with your motivation and carrying on with an existence of satisfaction and significance. A deliberate mentality includes moving toward existence with aim, lucidity, and concentration, and remaining associated with your feeling of direction and bearing, even notwithstanding difficulties or vulnerability. At the point when you develop a deliberate mentality, you tap into a profound well of inward strength, versatility, and clearness that engages you to explore life's promising and less promising times with beauty and reason.

To develop a deliberate outlook, begin by explaining your feeling of direction and vision for your life. Think about the main thing to you and what you desire to accomplish or contribute on the planet. Consider the effect you need to make and the heritage you need to abandon, and let these bits of knowledge guide your activities and choices in arrangement with your motivation.

Practice appreciation and care to remain present and participated in the occasion, appreciating the magnificence and overflow that encompasses you every day. Develop a feeling of stunningness and miracle for your general surroundings, and move toward every day with a feeling of interest, receptiveness, and appreciation for the valuable open doors and encounters that come your direction.

Participate in standard self-reflection and contemplation to remain associated with your qualities, interests, and yearnings. Put away opportunity for journaling, reflection, or calm examination to investigate your considerations, sentiments, and bits of knowledge, and gain lucidity on your objectives and needs. Utilize these snapshots of reflection to reaffirm your feeling of direction and course, and realign your activities and decisions with your most profound qualities and yearnings.

Encircle yourself with individuals who rouse and inspire you, and search out conditions and encounters that feed your feeling of direction and prosperity. Fabricate an encouraging group of people of companions, coaches, and similar people who share your qualities and desires, and rest on them for direction, consolation, and backing as you seek after your motivation.

By developing a deliberate outlook, you engage yourself to carry on with an existence of importance, satisfaction, and effect. Embrace every day as a valuable chance to line up with your motivation and have a constructive outcome on the planet, and confidence in your capacity to make a day to day existence that mirrors the genuine substance of what your identity is and a big motivator for you. With an intentional mentality as your aide, you open the possibility to carry on with an existence of enthusiasm, reason, and satisfaction, having a significant effect on your general surroundings.

| 8 |

Chapter 8: Manifesting Your Dreams

Picturing Achievement

Picturing achievement is a useful asset for showing your fantasies and objectives into the real world. Representation includes making striking mental pictures of the results you want, connecting each of your faculties to inspire the feelings and sensations related with accomplishing your fantasies. By consistently envisioning achievement, you adjust your psyche brain to your cognizant expectations, programming it to search out amazing open doors and make moves that draw you nearer to your objectives.

To rehearse perception, begin by saving devoted time every day to calm your psyche and spotlight on your fantasies and goals. Find a peaceful, agreeable space where you can unwind and loosen up, liberated from interruptions. Shut your eyes and envision yourself previously carrying on with the existence of your fantasies, encountering the entirety of the sights, sounds, scents, and sensations related with accomplishing your objectives.

Make a point by point mental image of your ideal result, envisioning yourself achieving your objectives with lucidity and accuracy. Envision yourself defeating hindrances, confronting difficulties with strength and assurance, and praising your triumphs with happiness and appreciation. Connect each of your faculties to make the representation as striking and vivid as could really be expected, permitting yourself to completely encounter the feelings and sensations related with accomplishing your fantasies.

Practice perception consistently, integrating it into your everyday daily schedule as an integral asset for programming your psyche mind for progress. Envision your objectives as currently refined, zeroing in on the positive feelings and sensations related with accomplishing them. Trust in the force of representation to adjust your contemplations, convictions, and activities with your cravings, and remain open to the open doors and synchronicities that emerge subsequently.

By picturing achievement, you actuate the pattern of good following good and polarize yourself to individuals, assets, and conditions that will uphold the indication of your fantasies. Embrace the act of perception as a useful asset for changing your fantasies into the real world, and confidence in your capacity to make the existence you want through the force of your viewpoints, convictions, and goals.

Rehearsing Appreciation and Overflow

Rehearsing appreciation and developing an outlook of overflow are fundamental components of showing your fantasies. Appreciation is the act of recognizing and valuing the favors, open doors, and overflow that as of now exist in your life, while overflow is the conviction that there is all that could possibly be needed to go around and that you have the right to get every one of the beneficial things life brings to the table.

To rehearse appreciation, begin by making a day to day propensity for remembering your good fortune and offering thanks for individuals, encounters, and open doors in your day to day existence. Keep an appreciation diary where you can record three things you're thankful for every day, regardless of how large or little. Set aside some margin to relish and value the overflow that encompasses you, from the magnificence of nature to the affection and backing of loved ones.

Develop an overflow outlook by moving your concentration from shortage and need to overflow and plausibility. Challenge restricting convictions about shortage and shamefulness, and attest your faith in your own deservingness and value to get every one of the favors and potential open doors life brings to the table. Trust in the universe's boundless ability to accommodate your requirements and wants, and embrace a demeanor of hope and receptiveness to getting overflow in the entirety of its structures.

Practice liberality and generosity toward others, knowing that by giving uninhibitedly of yourself, you free yourself up to getting considerably more overflow consequently. Share your time, gifts, and assets with others, and trust that your thoughtful gestures will be reimbursed many times over as favors and potential open doors that come your direction.

Remain open to the overflow that encompasses you and get the endowments and open doors that come your direction with appreciation and effortlessness. Trust in the force of appreciation and overflow to draw in a greater amount of what you want into your life, and realize that by developing these characteristics, you conform to the progression of flourishing and overflow that is dependably accessible to you.

Making A motivated Move

Making a motivated move is an essential move toward showing your fantasies into the real world. While perception and appreciation set up for indication, it is through activity that you rejuvenate your fantasies. Roused activity is activity that emerges from a position of arrangement with your most profound cravings and goals, directed by instinct, inward insight, and a feeling of direction.

To make a propelled move, begin by tuning into your instinct and internal direction. Calm your brain and stand by listening to the murmurs of your heart, focusing on the inconspicuous pokes and motivations that emerge inside you. Trust in your instinct to direct you toward the activities and decisions that are in arrangement with your fantasies and objectives, regardless of whether they might appear to be whimsical or dubious.

Develop a feeling of clearness and concentration around your objectives and goals, knowing precisely very thing you need to accomplish and why it is important to you. Set clear, explicit objectives that are lined up with your vision and values, and separate them into noteworthy advances that you can take toward their accomplishment. Remain focused on your objectives and aims, and take predictable, determined activity to carry them to completion.

Be available to open doors and synchronicities that emerge en route, believing that the universe is continuously contriving to help you in showing your fantasies. Focus on signs, images, and messages that might show up in surprising spots, and heed the direction they offer, regardless of whether it leads you down a way you hadn't expected.

Take strong, brave activity toward your fantasies, venturing outside your usual range of familiarity and embracing the obscure with confidence and certainty. Trust in your capacity to explore difficulties and hindrances with elegance and strength, realizing that each step you take carries you nearer to the acknowledgment of your fantasies.

By making an enlivened move, you conform to the progression of indication and outfit the force of your viewpoints, convictions, and expectations to make the existence you want. Embrace the excursion of making a motivated move as a chance for development, self-revelation, and strengthening, and confidence in your capacity to show your fantasies with boldness, assurance, and beauty.

Making A motivated Move

Making a motivated move is a basic move toward showing your fantasies and transforming your dreams into the real world. While perception and positive reasoning are useful assets for setting aims and explaining your longings, it is the moves you make in arrangement with those expectations that at last carry your fantasies to completion. Roused activity is activity that emerges from a position of instinct, inward insight, and arrangement with your most elevated reason and values.

To make a propelled move, begin by tuning into your instinct and internal direction to recognize the following stages on your way toward showing your fantasies. Calm your psyche and pay attention to the murmurs of your heart, focusing on any pokes, experiences, or motivations that emerge inside you. Trust in your inward insight to direct you toward the activities that are generally lined up with your longings and aims.

Be available to startling open doors and synchronicities that current themselves en route. Some of the time, the universe will convey you signs and messages that point you toward your fantasies, and it depends on you to perceive and immediately jump all over those chances when they emerge. Remain open, adaptable, and versatile to the progression of life, and take strong, gallant activity when everything looks good.

Separate your objectives into significant stages and make a game plan for accomplishing them. Recognize the particular assignments, assets, and backing you should rejuvenate your fantasies, and focus on taking predictable, centered activity toward your objectives every day. Trust in the force of little, steady moves toward draw you nearer to your fantasies, and praise every achievement en route.

Discharge connection to the result and give up to the course of sign. Believe that the universe has an arrangement for yourself and that everything is unfurling in divine timing. Relinquish the need to control each part of your excursion and give up to the progression of life, be-lieving that everything is turning out for your most elevated great.

By making a propelled move, you conform to the progression of creation and enable yourself to co-make your existence with the uni-verse. Embrace the excursion of sign with boldness, confidence, and trust, realizing that by heeding your internal direction and taking in-tense, motivated activity, you are establishing the groundwork for the acknowledgment of your fantasies.

Defeating Self-Restricting Convictions

Defeating self-restricting convictions is fundamental for showing your fantasies and opening your maximum capacity. Self-restricting convictions are negative or restricting convictions about yourself, your capacities, and your value to accomplish your objectives. These convictions can keep you away from making an enlivened move and seeking after your fantasies with certainty and conviction.

To defeat self-restricting convictions, begin by distinguishing and testing the convictions that are keeping you down. Focus on the negative considerations and self-talk that emerge to you, and notice any examples or subjects that arise. Find out if these convictions depend on the real world or essentially old molding and programming that never again serve you.

Work on reexamining negative convictions into really engaging and strong convictions that line up with your objectives and yearnings. Supplant self-restricting convictions with positive certifications and explanations that avow your value, deservingness, and capacity to accomplish your fantasies. Confirm your confidence in your own true capacity and ability to make the existence you want, and rehash these certifications consistently to build up them in your psyche mind.

Challenge yourself to step outside your usual range of familiarity and make moves that go against your self-restricting convictions. Drive yourself to attempt new things, face challenges, and seek after amazing open doors that challenge your apparent restrictions and grow your feeling of plausibility. Commend your victories en route, regardless of how little, and use them as proof to check your self-restricting convictions.

Search out help and direction from guides, mentors, or believed loved ones who can help you challenge and defeat your self-restricting convictions. Encircle yourself with individuals who have faith in your true capacity and urge you to seek after your fantasies with energy and reason. Rest on them for consolation, responsibility, and backing as you work to defeat your self-restricting convictions and manifest your fantasies.

By defeating self-restricting convictions, you enable yourself to step into your maximum capacity and make the existence you want. Embrace the excursion of self-revelation and self-awareness with boldness and assurance, realizing that by testing your self-restricting convictions and venturing outside your usual range of familiarity, you are establishing the groundwork for an existence of satisfaction, overflow, and reason.

Giving up to the Universe

Giving up to the universe is a strong practice for showing your fantasies and permitting them to unfurl effortlessly. Giving up doesn't mean surrendering or surrendering control; rather, it includes delivering connection to explicit results and confiding in the innate insight and knowledge of the universe to direct you toward your most noteworthy great. At the point when you give up, you let go of obstruction and permit the progression of life to convey you toward your fantasies, realizing that everything is unfurling precisely as it ought to.

To give up to the universe, begin by relinquishing the need to control each part of your excursion and believing that everything is occurring for your most noteworthy great. Discharge connection to explicit results and embrace a mentality of transparency, interest, and receptivity to the open doors and gifts that come your direction. Believe that the universe has an arrangement for yourself and that everything is unfurling in divine timing, regardless of whether it generally unfurl as per your assumptions or course of events.

Practice care and presence to remain grounded right now and develop a more profound feeling of trust and give up. Relinquish stresses over the future and second thoughts about the past, and spotlight on completely captivating with the present time and place. Embrace every second as a chance for development, learning, and association, and trust that by being completely present and drawn in, you conform to the progression of life and free yourself up to getting the direction and backing of the universe.

Discharge opposition and give up to the course of sign, permitting your fantasies to unfurl voluntarily and in their own ideal manner. Believe that the universe knows the best way for yourself and that everything is occurring precisely as it ought to help your most elevated great and development. Relinquish the need to compel or control results and on second thought give up to the insight and knowledge of the universe, knowing that when you give up, you fall in line with the normal progression of overflow and sign.

Embrace give up as an act of confidence, trust, and give up to the insight and knowledge of the universe, knowing that when you give up, you conform to the regular progression of overflow and indication. Give up is certainly not an indication of shortcoming yet rather a strong demonstration of boldness and confidence, permitting you to relinquish control and confidence in the more prominent insight and knowledge of the universe to direct you toward your most elevated great and the acknowledgment of your fantasies. Trust during the time spent give up, knowing that when you give up, you free yourself up to getting the endowments and open doors that the universe has coming up for you, and you fall in line with the progression of overflow and appearance that is generally accessible to you.

| 9 |

Chapter 9: Sustaining Personal Growth

Developing Mindfulness

Developing mindfulness is a central stage in supporting self-awareness and improvement. Mindfulness includes the capacity to perceive and grasp your own considerations, feelings, and ways of behaving, as well as their effect on yourself as well as other people. By fostering a more profound degree of mindfulness, you gain important bits of knowledge into your assets, shortcomings, values, and convictions, which empowers you to pursue more cognizant and deliberate decisions in arrangement with your self-awareness venture.

To develop mindfulness, begin by rehearsing care and self-reflection consistently. Put away opportunity every day to calm your psyche, tune into your internal contemplations and sentiments, and notice your considerations and feelings without judgment. Notice any examples or propensities in your reasoning and conduct, and investigate the hidden inspirations and convictions that drive them.

Journaling can be an integral asset for developing mindfulness. Record your considerations, sentiments, and encounters, and think about them with interest and transparency. Use journaling as a method for investigating your internal scene, gain clearness on your objectives and values, and recognize regions for development and improvement.

Look for criticism from others to acquire alternate points of view on yourself and your way of behaving. Ask confided in companions, relatives, or coaches for genuine criticism about your assets, shortcomings, and regions for development. Be available to getting valuable analysis and use it as a chance for development and self-revelation.

Practice self-sympathy and acknowledgment as you develop mindfulness. Embrace all parts of yourself, including your assets and defects, with consideration and empathy. Perceive that mindfulness is an excursion of constant development and learning, and show restraint toward yourself as you explore the promising and less promising times of self-revelation.

By developing mindfulness, you establish the groundwork for supportable self-awareness and advancement. As you develop how you might interpret yourself and your internal world, you gain more prominent clearness, understanding, and intelligence to explore life's difficulties and open doors with effortlessness and legitimacy. Embrace the excursion of mindfulness with interest, receptiveness, and empathy, knowing that by knowing yourself profoundly, you engage yourself to carry on with an existence of direction, significance, and satisfaction.

Embracing Deep rooted Learning

Embracing deep rooted learning is fundamental for supporting self-improvement and adjusting to the always changing scene of life. In a world that is continually developing, the capacity to master new abilities, get new information, and adjust to new conditions is vital for individual and expert achievement. Long lasting learning not just extends your points of view and upgrades your capacities, however it likewise cultivates a mentality of interest, development, and versatility that enables you to flourish in any climate.

To embrace long lasting learning, take on a development outlook that perspectives difficulties and mishaps as any open doors for learning and development. Develop a feeling of interest and receptiveness to new encounters, thoughts, and points of view, and move toward every day as a valuable chance to grow your insight and abilities.

Search out valuable open doors for formal and casual learning in different areas of interest. Take classes, studios, or online courses to extend how you might interpret points that interest you, and participate in independent learning through books, web recordings, and other instructive assets. Be proactive in searching out new encounters and difficulties that push you out of your usual range of familiarity and stretch your capacities.

Remain inquisitive and curious, getting clarification on pressing issues and looking for replies to extend how you might interpret your general surroundings. Encircle yourself with individuals who motivate and challenge you, and take part in significant discussions and discussions that animate your astuteness and expand your points of view.

Practice ceaseless personal growth by defining objectives for individual and expert development and effectively seeking after them. Separate your objectives into reasonable advances and make a steady move toward accomplishing them, praising your advancement en route.

Stay unassuming and open to criticism, perceiving that there is dependably space for development and improvement. Concede whenever you don't know something and search out chances to gain from other people who have ability in regions where you might need.

By embracing deep rooted learning, you develop an outlook of development, flexibility, and versatility that engages you to flourish in any circumstance. Embrace the excursion of learning with energy, interest, and a guarantee to individual and expert development, realizing that by constantly growing your insight and abilities, you open new open doors and opportunities for progress and satisfaction throughout everyday life.

Sustaining Strength

Supporting versatility is fundamental for supporting self-awareness and flourishing despite life's unavoidable difficulties and misfortunes. Versatility is the capacity to quickly return from affliction, conquer impediments, and adjust to change with strength and beauty. By developing flexibility, you develop inward fortitude, backbone, and close to home deftness that empower you to explore life's high points and low points with strength and assurance.

To sustain versatility, begin by reevaluating your point of view on difficulties and misfortunes. Rather than survey them as unfavorable obstructions or disappointments, consider them to be potential open doors for development, learning, and self-improvement. Embrace difficulties as significant opportunities for growth that reinforce your strength muscles and set you up for future difficulties.

Foster sound survival strategies for overseeing pressure and difficulty. Practice taking care of oneself exercises like activity, reflection, and investing time in nature to renew your energy and cultivate close to home prosperity. Develop major areas of strength for an organization of companions, relatives, and coaches who can give consolation, direction, and daily reassurance during troublesome times.

Assemble critical thinking abilities and versatile survival techniques to explore difficulties and mishaps actually. Separate issues into sensible advances and spotlight on finding viable arrangements instead of harping on the actual issue. Be proactive in searching out assets and backing to assist you with defeating deterrents and accomplish your objectives.

Practice self-sympathy and self-acknowledgment as you explore difficulties and misfortunes. Indulge yourself with generosity and understanding, and recognize your endeavors and progress, even notwithstanding difficulties. Develop a positive outlook that spotlights on your assets and versatility, as opposed to harping on apparent shortcomings or disappointments.

Embrace a development outlook that perspectives challenges as any open doors for learning and development. Embrace the conviction that you have the ability to gain and develop from each insight, regardless of how troublesome or difficult. Trust in your capacity to defeat deterrents and return more grounded and stronger than previously.

By supporting strength, you enable yourself to flourish despite affliction and support self-improvement over the long haul. Embrace the excursion of flexibility with boldness, persistence, and a readiness to gain and develop from each insight, realizing that by developing versatility, you develop internal fortitude and determination that empower you to explore life's difficulties with elegance and strength.

Sustaining Versatility

Supporting versatility is fundamental for supporting self-improvement, particularly despite misfortune and difficulties. Flexibility is the capacity to return from difficulties, adjust to change, and flourish notwithstanding affliction. By developing versatility, you foster the internal strength, fortitude, and adaptability to explore life's promising and less promising times with elegance and flexibility, empowering you to keep developing and advancing even in the most difficult conditions.

To support strength, begin by reevaluating mishaps and disappointments as any open doors for development and learning. Rather than review snags as inconceivable hindrances, consider them to be transitory difficulties that offer important examples and bits of knowledge. Take on an outlook of good faith and flexibility, confiding in your capacity to defeat difficulties and arise more grounded and stronger than previously.

Foster solid survival techniques for overseeing pressure and misfortune. Practice taking care of oneself strategies like activity, reflection, and care to decrease pressure and advance close to home prosperity. Fabricate serious areas of strength for an organization of companions, relatives, and coaches who can give consolation, direction, and backing during troublesome times.

Develop a feeling of viewpoint and appreciation, zeroing in on the gifts and open doors that exist even amidst misfortune. Keep an uplifting perspective and search for silver linings in testing circumstances, perceiving that each mishap is a chance for development and change.

Foster critical thinking abilities and versatile ways of dealing with hardship or stress to explore difficulties and mishaps actually. Separate issues into sensible advances and foster activity plans for tending to them. Remain adaptable and receptive, ready to adjust your methodology on a case by case basis to conquer snags and accomplish your objectives.

By supporting versatility, you foster the internal strength, fortitude, and adaptability to explore life's difficulties with elegance and flexibility. Embrace the excursion of self-improvement with mental fortitude, flexibility, and assurance, realizing that by developing versatility, you engage yourself to conquer hindrances, adjust to change, and keep developing and advancing notwithstanding misfortune.

Point 4: Developing Sound Propensities

Developing solid propensities is fundamental for supporting self-improvement and prosperity in all everyday issues. Sound propensities envelop many ways of behaving that advance physical, mental, and profound prosperity, from normal activity and adjusted sustenance to satisfactory rest and stress the board strategies. By focusing on taking care of oneself and developing solid propensities, you establish the groundwork for practical self-awareness and satisfaction.

To develop solid propensities, begin by focusing on taking care of oneself and making your physical, mental, and close to home prosperity a first concern. Lay out a customary work-out schedule that incorporates a blend of cardiovascular, strength preparing, and adaptability activities to advance actual wellness and by and large wellbeing. Eat a reasonable eating routine wealthy in organic products, vegetables, entire grains, and lean proteins to fuel your body and backing ideal wellbeing and essentialness.

Focus on rest by laying out a steady rest plan and pursuing great rest cleanliness routines, for example, restricting screen time before bed and making a loosening up sleep time schedule. Hold back nothing nine hours of value rest every night to help physical and psychological well-being and prosperity.

Practice pressure the executives methods like care, contemplation, profound breathing, and moderate muscle unwinding to diminish pressure and advance unwinding. Set aside a few minutes for exercises that give you pleasure and unwinding, like investing energy in nature, seeking after side interests and interests, and interfacing with friends and family.

Focus on mental and close to home wellbeing by looking for help from emotional well-being experts when required and rehearsing self-empathy and taking care of oneself. Put down stopping points and focus on exercises that feed and restore your brain, body, and soul.

By developing solid propensities, you make areas of strength for a for supported self-improvement and prosperity. Embrace the excursion of taking care of oneself and sound living with responsibility, consistency, and empathy, realizing that by focusing on your physical, mental, and close to home prosperity, you engage yourself to carry on with an existence of essentialness, satisfaction, and reason.

Encouraging Significant Associations

Encouraging significant associations with others is an essential part of supporting self-awareness and prosperity. People are social animals naturally, and our associations with others assume a critical part in forming our encounters, discernments, and healthy identity. By supporting bona fide and significant associations with others, we enhance our lives, extend how we might interpret ourselves and our general surroundings, and make a feeling of having a place and backing that supports us through life's difficulties and wins.

To encourage significant associations, focus on building and keeping up with associations with individuals who share your qualities, interests, and goals. Encircle yourself with companions, relatives, and associates who elevate and motivate you, and who support you in your self-improvement venture. Put investment in developing these connections, sustaining them with care, thoughtfulness, and veritable premium.

Practice undivided attention and compassion in your cooperations with others, looking to figure out their viewpoints, sentiments, and encounters without judgment or analysis. Show empathy, consideration, and understanding toward others, and proposition backing and consolation when required. Be available and completely participated in your cooperations, offering others your unified consideration and causing them to feel seen, heard, and esteemed.

Take part in significant discussions and exercises that cultivate association and closeness with others. Share your considerations, sentiments, and encounters straightforwardly and legitimately, and urge others to do likewise. Track down normal interests and interests that you can investigate together, whether it's through common leisure activities, interests, or objectives.

Practice pardoning and compromise in your connections, perceiving that struggles and misconceptions are a characteristic piece of human communication. Apologize when you commit errors and to excuse others when they hurt or frustrate you. Relinquish hard feelings and feelings of disdain, and spotlight rather on developing adoration, empathy, and figuring out in your connections.

By cultivating significant associations with others, you make an encouraging group of people of adoration, consolation, and motivation that supports you through life's difficulties and wins. Embrace the excursion of building and sustaining bona fide associations with receptiveness, weakness, and realness, realizing that by associating with others in significant ways, you enhance your own life and add to the prosperity and bliss of everyone around you.

| 10 |

Chapter 10: Conclusion

Pondering Your Excursion

As you arrive at the finish of this book, it's vital for pause for a minute to ponder the excursion you've left upon. Pondering your self-awareness venture permits you to stop and recognize the headway you've made, the difficulties you've survived, and the bits of knowledge you've acquired en route. Set aside some margin to respect your development and improvement, perceiving the mental fortitude, commitment, and versatility it took to get to where you are today.

Start your appearance by considering the objectives you set for yourself toward the start of your excursion. Consider how far you've come in accomplishing those objectives and praise the achievements you've arrived at en route. Celebrate the enormous accomplishments as well as the little triumphs and snapshots of development that might have slipped by everyone's notice.

Then, ponder the difficulties and deterrents you experienced on your excursion. Consider how you explored these difficulties and what examples you gained from them. Perceive the strength and versatility you showed even with misfortune, and recognize the development and astuteness that came from defeating deterrents.

Consider the bits of knowledge and disclosures you've made about yourself all through your self-awareness venture. Ponder the qualities, convictions, and needs that have arisen or moved because of your encounters. Consider how your view of yourself and your general surroundings have advanced, and embrace the new points of view and understandings you've acquired.

At long last, pause for a minute to offer thanks for the excursion you've been on and the encounters you've had en route. Offer thanks for the illustrations took in, the development experienced, and the valuable open doors for self-disclosure and change. Develop a feeling of appreciation for individuals, assets, and emotionally supportive networks that have added to your development and improvement.

By thinking about your self-improvement venture, you honor the headway you've made, coordinate the examples learned, and set up for proceeded with development and advancement later on. Embrace this chance to stop, reflect, and praise your excursion, realizing that the bits of knowledge acquired will proceed to direct and motivate you on your way ahead.

Observing Accomplishments

As you close your excursion of self-improvement, it's urgent to require the investment to praise your accomplishments en route. Commending your accomplishments isn't just about perceiving your triumphs; it's tied in with regarding the difficult work, devotion, and mental fortitude that have carried you to this point. Whether you've arrived at critical achievements or gained little yet significant headway, every accomplishment is a demonstration of your strength and obligation to self-awareness.

Start by distinguishing and recognizing the accomplishments you've made all through your excursion. Ponder the objectives you set for yourself at the beginning and consider how far you've come in accomplishing them. Praise the headway you've made, regardless of how huge or little, and perceive the work and persistence it took to arrive at every achievement.

Celebrate the substantial results as well as the self-awareness and improvement you've encountered en route. Recognize the inward changes, changes in outlook, and newly discovered qualities that have arisen because of your excursion. Commend the snapshots of fortitude, versatility, and self-revelation that have added to your development and improvement.

Get some margin to respect your accomplishments such that feels significant to you. This could include imparting your triumphs to friends and family, indulging yourself with a unique prize or guilty pleasure, or just pausing for a minute to relax in the feeling of achievement and pride that comes from arriving at your objectives. Anything that structure it takes, commending your accomplishments is a significant chance to recognize your advancement and construct trust in your capacity to keep developing and developing.

Utilize this snapshot of festivity to develop a feeling of appreciation for the excursion you've been on and the encounters you've had en route. Offer thanks for the help, consolation, and assets that have helped you along your way, and for the potential open doors for development and self-disclosure that have enhanced your life.

By commending your accomplishments, you honor your advancement as well as fuel your inspiration and certainty to keep pushing ahead on your self-awareness venture. Embrace this chance to recognize your victories, offer thanks for your excursion, and gather speed for the following section of development and improvement in your life.

Observing Accomplishments

As you approach the finish of this extraordinary excursion, it's pivotal to pause for a minute to praise your accomplishments. Praising your achievements isn't just a method for recognizing your diligent effort and devotion yet in addition a strong method for supporting your advancement and lift your certainty. Regardless of how huge or little your accomplishments might appear, every one addresses a forward-moving step on your way to self-improvement and satisfaction.

Start by distinguishing and considering the accomplishments you've made all through your excursion. Consider the objectives you set for yourself toward the start of this cycle and assess the headway you've made toward accomplishing them. Commend the achievements you've reached, whether it's finishing a difficult job, conquering a trepidation, or rolling out a positive improvement in your life.

Carve out opportunity to recognize the work and assurance it took to arrive at every achievement. Perceive the obstructions you looked en route and the strength you showed in defeating them. Celebrate the outcome as well as the actual excursion, embracing the illustrations learned and the development experienced en route.

Track down significant ways of praising your accomplishments that impact you actually. This could be basically as straightforward as indulging yourself with something you appreciate, for example, an extraordinary dinner or a loosening up free day, or as intricate as tossing a festival with companions and friends and family. Pick exercises that mirror your qualities and needs and that honor the meaning of your achievements.

Share your accomplishments with other people who have upheld and empowered you en route. Offer thanks to companions, relatives, coaches, or associates who have applauded you and offered direction and backing when required. Get together to celebrate, relaxing in the delight and pride of your common achievements.

By commending your accomplishments, you recognize your advancement as well as support your confidence in yourself and your capacity to succeed. Embrace this chance to perceive and respect your persistent effort and commitment, realizing that every accomplishment carries you one bit nearer to carrying on with the existence you want.

Setting Goals for What's to come

As you arrive at the finish of this groundbreaking excursion, it's normal to start pondering the future and what lies ahead. Setting aims for what's in store permits you to channel the energy and energy you've acquired from your self-improvement venture into substantial objectives and goals for the days, weeks, and months to come. By setting aims, you explain your vision for the future and focus on making a move toward the existence you want.

Start by considering the bits of knowledge and examples you've acquired from your self-awareness venture hitherto. Consider how your encounters have molded your qualities, needs, and yearnings, and utilize this information to illuminate your aims for what's in store. Ponder what makes the biggest difference to you and what you need to make or accomplish in the space of wellbeing, connections, profession, self-improvement, and then some.

Recognize explicit objectives and targets that line up with your qualities and desires. Your objectives might be present moment or long haul, huge or little, however they ought to be significant and applicable to you actually. Be clear and explicit about what you need to achieve and why it is important to you, and consider separating bigger objectives into more modest, reasonable moves toward make them more reachable.

Whenever you've distinguished your expectations and objectives, make a game plan for accomplishing them. Separate every objective into noteworthy stages and lay out a course of events for fulfillment. Consider any assets or emotionally supportive networks you might have to accomplish your objectives and make an arrangement for getting to them.

Remain adaptable and receptive as you pursue your goals, staying open to new open doors and potential outcomes that might emerge en route. Adjust your objectives and plans on a case by case basis in light of changing conditions or new bits of knowledge. Trust in your capacity to explore the excursion ahead with mental fortitude, versatility, and assurance.

By setting goals for the future, you conform to the vision of the existence you want and focus on making a move toward making it a reality. Embrace this amazing chance to explain your objectives and desires, realizing that by setting goals and making a move, you engage yourself to make the daily routine you genuinely need to experience.

Observing Accomplishments

As you approach the finish of your excursion to self-revelation, it's essential to pause for a minute to commend your accomplishments. Praising your accomplishments is something other than a gesture of congratulations; it's a valuable chance to recognize the difficult work, commitment, and fortitude it took to arrive at your objectives. Regardless of how enormous or little your achievements might appear, every one addresses a huge step in the right direction on your way to self-improvement and change.

Start by making a rundown of the multitude of accomplishments you've made all through your excursion. These could incorporate arriving at explicit achievements, beating difficulties, or rolling out sure improvements in your day to day existence. Carve out opportunity to think about every accomplishment and the work it took to achieve it. Perceive the headway you've made and the hindrances you've beaten en route.

Whenever you've arranged your rundown of accomplishments, find opportunity to praise every one. Indulge yourself with something uniquely great — a little guilty pleasure or a significant prize that respects your diligent effort and devotion. Share your accomplishments with other people who have upheld you on your excursion, whether it's companions, relatives, guides, or partners. Get together to celebrate and relax in the delight of your achievements.

As well as praising your previous accomplishments, carve out opportunity to recognize your true capacity for future achievement. Perceive that your accomplishments are separated occasions as well as are proof of your capacities and potential for proceeded with development and achievement. Utilize your previous accomplishments as inspiration to define new objectives and seek after new dreams, realizing that you have what it takes, flexibility, and assurance to conquer any impediments that might come your direction.

By praising your accomplishments, you confirm your value and ability to make the existence you want. You perceive the headway you've made and the snags you've survived, and you develop a feeling of satisfaction and trust in yourself and your capacities. Embrace this chance to praise your excursion and the amazing individual you've become en route.

Setting Goals for What's to come

As you close your excursion of self-disclosure, it's fundamental to require investment to set expectations for what's to come. Setting expectations permits you to explain your vision for the existence you need to make and focus on making a move toward your objectives. Your goals act as a guide for your future, directing your choices and activities as you proceed to develop and advance.

Start by thinking about the bits of knowledge and examples you've acquired from your excursion of self-disclosure. Consider how your encounters have molded your qualities, convictions, and needs, and imagine the existence you need to make for yourself pushing ahead. What are your expectations, dreams, and yearnings for what's in store? What is it that you need to accomplish, insight, or make in the days, months, and years to come?

When you have clearness on your goals, record them in a diary or on a piece of paper. Be explicit and concrete in your aims, zeroing in on what you need to appear in your life as opposed to what you need to stay away from. Utilize positive language and insistences to build up your aims and conform to the energy of appearance.

With your aims explained, focus on making a move toward your objectives every day. Separate your expectations into significant stages and make an arrangement for accomplishing them. Set cutoff times and achievements to keep yourself responsible and keep tabs on your development en route. Remain adaptable and open to new open doors and encounters that might emerge as you pursue your goals.

At last, develop a feeling of trust and confidence during the time spent indication. Believe that the universe has an arrangement for yourself and that everything is unfurling precisely as it ought to. Give any connection over to explicit results and stay open to the conceivable outcomes that current themselves en route. By setting aims and making an enlivened move, you fall in line with the progression of overflow and sign, and you engage yourself to make the existence you want.

As you set goals for the future, recall that you have the ability to make the existence you need. Trust in yourself and your capacities, and realize that by setting clear goals and making a steady move, you can show your fantasies and carry on with an existence of direction, energy, and satisfaction. Embrace this chance to imagine the future you want and focus on doing whatever it may take to carry it to completion.

Proceeding with Your Development

As you arrive at the finish of this groundbreaking excursion, it's vital to perceive that self-improvement is a long lasting interaction. Your excursion of self-disclosure doesn't end here; it's a continuous excursion of learning, development, and advancement that keeps on unfurling as time passes. Focusing on proceeding with your development past the pages of this book is fundamental for extending your mindfulness, growing your true capacity, and carrying on with an existence of satisfaction and reason.

To proceed with your development, embrace a mentality of long lasting learning and personal growth. Remain inquisitive and liberal, searching out new encounters, difficulties, and valuable open doors for development. Put away opportunity every day for self-reflection and thoughtfulness, and keep on investigating groundbreaking thoughts, points of view, and practices that impact you.

Take what you've gained from this excursion and coordinate it into your regular routine. Apply the bits of knowledge, apparatuses, and methods you've acquired to defeat difficulties, seek after your objectives, and live in arrangement with your qualities and reason. Step outside your usual range of familiarity and attempt new things, realizing that development frequently requires pushing past your apparent restrictions and embracing additional opportunities.

Search out open doors for individual and expert turn of events, whether it's through proper schooling, studios, courses, or independent learning. Put resources into yourself and your development, realizing that the information and abilities you get will work well for you on your excursion toward turning into your best self.

Encircle yourself with individuals who motivate and uphold your development, and develop connections that inspire and engage you. Interface with tutors, mentors, and similar people who can offer direction, backing, and consolation as you proceed to advance and develop.

Share your excursion with others and be available to gaining from their encounters and points of view also.

At long last, make sure to be patient and empathetic with yourself as you proceed with your development process. Development takes time, exertion, and devotion, and experiencing mishaps and difficulties en route is regular. Embrace these difficulties as any open doors for development and learning, and confidence in your capacity to conquer them with strength and assurance.

By focusing on proceeding with your development, you insist your obligation to carrying on with an existence of direction, enthusiasm, and satisfaction. Embrace the excursion of self-revelation with energy, interest, and an eagerness to learn and develop every day. Realize that by remaining focused on your development process, you enable yourself to make the existence you want and merit — an existence of significance, satisfaction, and limitless potential.

www.ingramcontent.com/pod-product-compliance
Lightning Source LLC
Chambersburg PA
CBHW031331130726
47988CB00007B/3091